Music Booster Manual

Published in partnership with
MENC: The National Association for Music Education
Frances S. Ponick, Executive Editor

Rowman & Littlefield Education
Lanham • New York • Toronto • Plymouth, UK

Published in partnership with
MENC: The National Association for Music Education

Published in the United States of America
by Rowman & Littlefield Education
A Division of Rowman & Littlefield Publishers, Inc.
A wholly owned subsidiary of The Rowman & Littlefield Publishing Group, Inc.
4501 Forbes Boulevard, Suite 200, Lanham, Maryland 20706
www.rowmaneducation.com

Estover Road
Plymouth PL6 7PY
United Kingdom

Copyright © 1989 by MENC: The National Association for Music Education
First Roman & Littlefield Education printing 2008

All rights reserved. No part of this publication may be reproduced, stored in a retrieval system, or transmitted in any form or by any means, electronic, mechanical, photocopying, recording, or otherwise, without the prior permission of the publisher.

British Library Cataloguing in Publication Information Available

Library of Congress Cataloging-in-Publication Data

ISBN-13: 978-0-940796-68-3 (pbk. : alk. paper)
ISBN-10: 0-940796-68-6 (pbk. : alk. paper)

∞™ The paper used in this publication meets the minimum requirements of American National Standard for Information Sciences—Permanence of Paper for Printed Library Materials, ANSI/NISO Z39.48-1992.
Manufactured in the United States of America.

Contents

Acknowledgments iv
Introduction v
1. Starting a Booster Group 1
2. Booster Organization 3
3. Meetings 6
4. Budgeting 8
5. Fundraising 11
6. Travel 16
7. Publicity 24
8. Communications 27
Appendix 1: Constitution and Bylaws 31
Appendix 2: Uniform Management 47

Acknowledgments

MENC: The National Association for Music Education would like to thank the following individuals and groups for their contributions to this manual:

Sandy Feldstein, Alfred Publishing Company

Charles Hoffer, University of Florida, Gainesville; president, Music Educators National Conference, 1988–1990

"Buz" Lowman, Owner, Central Travel of Silver Spring, Maryland

Lewis "Skip" Norcott, Music Department Chairman, Governor Mifflin Schools, Shillington, Pennsylvania

C. Dean Streator, Chairman, Music Booster Affiliates, Pennsylvania Music Educators Association

Mel Tobes, Regional Sales Manager (retired), Helen Grace Chocolates

Larry D. Williams, Bozeman Public Schools, Bozeman, Montana

Introduction

Good music programs inspire. They inspire not only students, they also inspire parents and community members. Because of this, music has a resource rare among the academic disciplines: adults who are willing to give their time and energy in its support.

This manual is intended to help music educators focus that energy by setting up, guiding, and working with a booster organization. Some of the information is directed primarily toward the music teacher, and some is for the boosters themselves. Some of the procedures described will be most appropriate for large organizations, but even the smallest groups will benefit from considering the principles behind the processes.

Before you get started in organizing a booster group, here are some things to think about.

- The booster program should always be thought of as an addition. The funds it raises are not a replacement for school funding to justified programs. Rather, it provides means for students to have music experiences beyond what the school can supply.
- The goal of a booster program is to assist and support the music educator so that he or she can maintain a music program that will be educational, enjoyable, and rewarding. But its authority should never reach into the content and priorities of the music program.
- A booster group is a music education advocacy group. When possible, it should be involved in supporting the entire music program, not just the chorus or marching band. After all, these are community members who have seen how important the arts are in children's educations and in their school experiences.
- When you are very active in fundraising, you need to be more aware than ever of your relationship with the community. Fundraising can be viewed as a form of supplemental taxation.

MENC: The National Association for Music Education recognizes the importance and dedication of booster organizations. Their efforts have allowed thousands of students to have some of the most thrilling experiences of their school lives. It is hoped that the information contained in this manual will assist in starting new groups and improving the efficiency of established groups. Music booster workshops, which are often offered by state music educators associations, are another important source of information. If you have any questions or ideas, contact MENC: The National Association for Music Education, Music Booster Information, 1806 Robert Fulton Drive, Reston, VA 20191-4348.

1
Starting a Booster Group

Getting a booster group off to a good start is largely a matter of communication and cooperation. If parents, administrators, and the music director are aware right from the beginning of the need for a booster group, the kind of activities it will engage in, and its goals, there will be less resistance and fewer misunderstandings later.

BEFORE THE FIRST MEETING

As the music director, your first step will be to let the school administration know about your plans. Explain carefully the kinds of things the booster group will do—and the kinds of things it won't do. Invite members of the administrative staff to booster planning sessions. If they have strong opinions (pro or con) about the formation of a booster group, you should know about them and they should be aired.

Notice who your supportive parents are: those who are always at concerts, those who volunteer when you put out a call for help, or those who have approached you about helping out. Arrange an informal meeting with four or five of these parents (or other interested individuals in the community) to discuss the formation of a booster group. Explain your need for parent boosters, what areas of your program would benefit from their assistance, the kinds of tasks and responsibilities they might be asked to take on, and the goals you have in mind for them and for the students. With the help of this core group, develop a plan for establishing and organizing the group and for recruiting members.

Make a list of parents who would make good officers and contact them about serving. The standard slate of officers includes a president, a vice president, a secretary (perhaps both a corresponding and a recording secretary), and a treasurer. Some, if not all, of those being considered will be a part of the small group you've assembled.

GENERAL MEETING

Choose a date for the first general meeting to explain your purpose and plans to all parents. Announce the meeting in a school or department newsletter, newspaper, concert program, or flyer sent home with students (keeping in mind that many flyers don't actually make it into the hands of parents). Have each of those who have agreed to help call at least five other interested people and invite them personally to the meeting.

Meet with those who have agreed to serve as officers before the general meeting. Plan what will be discussed, including purpose, membership, policies, long- and short-term goals, and activities. At the first general meeting, you will want to have the slate of officers elected or approved. You may also want to establish committees to deal with such things as ways and means, publicity, bylaws, telephone, travel, and a newsletter. You may want to select your first committee chairs the same way you selected officers.

OTHER CONSIDERATIONS

As soon as possible after the booster group becomes organized, establish a set of bylaws that clearly state purposes, goals, and responsibilities.

Before the organization collects any dues or raises its first dollar, open a bank account in the name of the group. Always keep booster funds separate from school funds. Never put a booster account in one person's name. A checking account works best with two signatures required. This means at least two officers, and preferably the entire executive committee, must approve the expenditure.

Consider incorporating. Advantages include being able to formally establish nonprofit and tax-exempt status. The booster group will be required to file annual federal and state tax returns and may be subject to an audit, but it will be exempt from paying income tax on earnings and possibly sales tax on purchases. One of the most important advantages is the perpetual protection of all involved. Consult an attorney or accountant. (Refer to the next section, on organization, for more information.)

2
Booster Organization

A successful business stimulates the productivity of its employees through salary, benefits, and incentives. But a booster program, which depends on volunteers, must stimulate the enthusiasm of its supporters by providing a clear vision of the good their efforts are achieving and by not wasting their time. Proper planning and organization, right from the start, are central to fulfilling this need.

BYLAWS

The goal of a booster program is to provide the music director with assistance and support that will allow him or her to develop an educational, enjoyable, and rewarding music program. Bylaws can provide operational guidelines toward that end. They are the rules adopted by an organization for management of its internal affairs. They should encompass the organization's purpose, membership, authorities, financial affairs, meetings, means for change, and parliamentary procedures. The bylaws should be formally approved by the full membership. (See Appendix 1 for a sample.)

INCORPORATION

There are a number of benefits to be gained by incorporating a booster group. An incorporated organization has the advantages of limited liability and perpetual existence. In addition, the establishment of a corporation can provide a clear definition of the framework and structure of the organization. It also will resolve questions about the purpose of the organization and its stability.

You will want to consult an attorney (who may be willing to donate his or her services) if you decide you want to incorporate. Although the steps for incorporation vary from state to state, they generally include the following:

Name of organization. Determine from the appropriate state authority the availability of the name selected for the organization and place it on reserve.

Articles of incorporation. Draft and file the articles of incorporation. Each state has a statute governing their content. In general, the following subjects are covered:

- Name of the corporation
- Duration of its existence

- Purpose
- Location of the initial office
- Name and address of the initial registered agent
- Names and addresses of the initial board of directors (usually three)
- Names and addresses of the incorporators (usually three)

Officers. Hold an organizational meeting of the initial board of directors to elect officers and to make other organizational decisions.

FUNCTIONAL RELATIONSHIPS

It's important to establish responsibility guidelines for the music director, booster organization, and school administration.

Music director. Basic responsibility for the music program is in the hands of the music director. He or she decides its content, plans curriculum and activities, selects music, and formulates policy and philosophy (following school guidelines). He or she also writes the budget and, of course, teaches, rehearses, and directs. The director is also responsible for identifying areas for expansion and improvement.

A primary responsibility of the music director in his or her relationship with the booster organization is to be sure that fundraising projects do not conflict with school policies or music program activities.

Boosters. The boosters organization must identify ways it can support the music program. This will often mean developing, managing, and implementing fundraising projects. Usually these projects are to buy items or finance projects that might be thought of as beyond the "baseline" curriculum: awards, banquets, special equipment, or trips. Booster groups might purchase items such as special music arrangements, stationery, risers, stands, tuners, banners and flags, duplicating equipment, or percussion supplies. It is to be hoped that the baseline curriculum is financially supported by the school, but in some cases booster assistance may be required to buy basic items such as instruments or music.

Boosters also typically provide assistance in chaperoning activities, sponsoring social events, making costumes, caring for uniforms or robes, and transporting students.

Generally, *what* the boosters purchase is largely the responsibility of the music director. *How* they raise the money necessary is largely the responsibility of the boosters. It is the responsibility of the director to provide timely information to the boosters concerning fundraising or volunteer man-hour needs. It is the responsibility of the boosters to schedule their fundraising and support activities so they will meet music program needs and to determine the degree of support that can be provided in the short or long term.

Administration. The school administration usually sets general policies concerning travel, time students can spend out of school, and fundraising projects associated with school programs. It is responsible for providing all basic supplies and equipment necessary for an adequate school music program and for providing facilities, instructors, instruments, music, uniforms/robes, and equipment. It is important that the funds raised by boosters always be viewed as supplemental to the funds provided by the school.

EXECUTIVE BOARD

The executive board, made up of officers and committee chairs, plans and implements booster activities. As a general rule, the membership on the executive board should represent a ratio of one member to every ten students in the program. The expertise and experience of the parent should be considered when making appointments to the board; however, an overriding qualification is the ability to deal with people in a positive manner.

President. The president is the chief executive officer of the organization and is responsible for all its actions. He or she provides the day-to-day liaison among the boosters, the director, and the school administration. He or she selects appointed members of the executive board.

Vice president. The vice president is the principal assistant to the president. He or she acts on behalf of the president and performs the president's duties when he or she is absent. In addition, he or she is assigned specific duties, such as managing a festival or tour or representing the organization on the state level and reporting to the executive board on state items.

Secretary. The secretary provides and maintains records of official acts of the organization. The secretary also develops and maintains the membership list.

Treasurer. The primary responsibility of the treasurer is to keep accurate financial records for the organization. The treasurer is also responsible for all authorized disbursements of the organization and reports to the organization on its financial condition. The treasurer is a member of the budget committee.

Trip coordinator. The trip coordinator is responsible, under the guidance of the music director, for trip planning, transportation, lodging, meals, itinerary, health information, and other administrative details.

COMMITTEES

Hospitality. This committee handles activities such as the hosting of visitors and providing refreshments for meetings. (See Chapter 3.)

Budget. This committee includes the music director, president, treasurer, and the ways and means committee chairman. It takes the director's proposed program and prepares the budgetary estimate for each element, making recommendations to the executive board and presenting the budget, as approved by the board, to the organization. (See Chapter 4.)

Ways and Means. The ways and means committee develops the plan for raising funds to support the budget and manages fundraising programs. (See Chapter 5.)

Chaperons. This committee develops and maintains a list of those who have volunteered for chaperon duty and assists in conducting the orientation and training of chaperons. Actual selection of the chaperons is a task assigned to the director and the trip coordinator. (See Chapter 6.)

Publicity. The publicity committee maintains contact with radio and television stations and newspapers and finds other ways of stimulating community interest. Activities such as producing a boosters yearbook might be a duty of this committee. (See Chapter 7.)

Newsletter. This committee produces the newsletter, which is the principal tool in recognizing student and parent contributions and accomplishments. The newsletter keeps members and others abreast of the total program activities and needs on a regular basis. (See Chapter 8.)

Telephone. The telephone committee provides rapid communications to parents and students. (See Chapter 8).

Uniforms or robes. This committee is responsible for fitting, issuing, maintaining, and keeping the inventory for uniforms or robes. (See Appendix 2.)

Other regular committees. Regular and continuing functions (such as selling at a concession stand) are usually better handled when they are separated from other activities and given the full-time attention of a committee. Additional committees might also be established for groups such as a band's auxiliary units or a swing or show choir.

3
Meetings

There are several things boosters can do to enhance participation and attendance at meetings. When establishing a meeting date, consider school and community activities that might conflict. Publicize the meeting well in advance so families can plan around the date.

At the meeting, provide refreshments, even if only coffee and tea. If possible, provide student musical entertainment (this also gives students performance experience). Have sign-up sheets for volunteer workers. Make personal contact with as many people in attendance as possible. Speak, shake hands, issue compliments, be cheerful and positive.

Pace and focus are very important. The president is responsible for maintaining control and keeping the meeting on schedule. When discussion of a subject has a slow start, questions such as, "Does anyone have any prior experience with this?" or "Can anyone suggest the basis or facts that we should be considering to put this subject in proper perspective?" should prompt member contributions. To stimulate further discussion, statements such as, "Let's hear from those who have been listening to the opinions presented so far," or "What other aspects of the subject should we be considering?" are usually helpful.

To divert attention from someone who has been dominating a discussion, try a statement like, "The ideas offered by _____ are very interesting. Can someone else add to or provide comments on them?"

Finally, a little humor goes a long way. A light approach to a touchy subject will facilitate positive interaction.

EXECUTIVE BOARD MEETINGS

The executive board is the booster organization's management team. It should gather monthly throughout the year, about a week before the general membership meeting. The executive board meeting is the means by which the organization's affairs are coordinated. It is important that all members of the executive board participate.

Agenda. The agenda is the president's responsibility, but the director's input is also important. This meeting provides a good opportunity to meet with the director in a way that ensures that he or she won't be interrupted during the school day.

Each functional division of the boosters' support program should be addressed on the agenda, and events that will occur within 90 to 120 days should be discussed. The following order of business may prove useful:
1. The president calls the meeting to order and makes opening remarks about the meeting agenda and upcoming events in the next several months. This should not be interrupted for discussion.
2. The secretary reads the minutes of the previous meeting, and the board approves or corrects.
3. The treasurer gives the financial report that will be presented to the general membership.
4. Other members of the executive board give committee reports including follow-ups on completed activities and recommendations for improvements and recognition, status of current activities, and identification of any approval or assistance needed to accomplish current tasks.

GENERAL MEMBERSHIP MEETING

The general membership meeting is the most important tool in developing and maintaining a successful booster program. It provides communication and stimulation of the organization. The conduct of the meeting must convey the message that the organization is on course with its goals. Every meeting must be run in a way that keeps to the point and avoids wandering general discussion. Meetings should be held regularly (for example, on the first Monday of each month).

The agenda for the general meeting, based on material covered at the executive board meeting, should be prepared by the president. A typical agenda might include the following:
1. The minutes: read by the secretary and approved or corrected by the members.
2. The treasurer's report.
3. The music director's report.
4. The executive board members' report on completed, current, and future activities.
5. A discussion and, if possible, resolution and closing of old business.
6. The introduction of new business in order of priority.
7. When all discussion is completed or tabled, the president's summary and closing of the meeting.

SPECIAL MEETINGS

Special meetings should be used to address subjects that would consume an unusual amount of time. An example would be a meeting to decide on making a commitment to purchase new uniforms.

An announcement should be made at the membership meeting and through the newsletter and telephone committee that a special meeting will be held to cover the actions and recommendations of the committee managing the special project. The announcement should indicate the actions that are to be considered at the meeting.

Agenda. The typical agenda for a special meeting would be as follows:
1. Introduce the subject, explain the purpose of the meeting, and outline the agenda.
2. Present background information and reports by appropriate committee members.
3. Present options and committee recommendations.
4. Call for a motion.
5. Entertain questions and discussion.
6. Call for the question and vote.
7. Summarize actions to be taken as a result of the membership decision.

4
Budgeting

The road to failure is paved with good intentions and bad budgets. Time spent in thinking out the budget, presenting it clearly, and living up to it will pay off in the availability of items most needed by the music program and in a spirit of effectiveness in the ranks of booster volunteers. The budgeting process is an integrated effort incorporating input from the director and the school administration as well as the boosters' executive board.

A booster group must recognize the immediate and long-range requirements of the organizations it supports and then set up a logical sequence of achievable goals. Careful planning will enhance the ability of the boosters to ensure staff, funds, and equipment necessary for a successful music program.

PROGRAM ASSESSMENT

Before the budget process begins, the music director should determine the program goals and objectives and the minimum program size necessary to meet the basic goals. This becomes the baseline program, which should usually be within the level of support provided by the school (but may require additional support from the booster program).

The director is also responsible for identifying the goals for growth beyond the baseline and priorities for accomplishing these goals. The following items should be considered in the program assessment.

Staff. Full-time teaching staff, part-time assistants and specialists, and office staff are the responsibility of the school. There may, however, be some exceptions. With the approval of the music director and school administration, boosters may want to supply funds for private instructors, section coaches, professional accompanists, choreographers, or show choir specialists. They may want to supply some volunteer office assistance, especially if a special project such as a festival has caused extra clerical work.

Physical plant and equipment. Most of the items included in this category should be covered by the school budget. Again, however, the boosters may have a role in upgrading facilities such as rehearsal areas, practice rooms, storage spaces, and auditoriums. They may also be asked to purchase uniforms or robes, instruments, or special music.

Travel. Usually a school or music department budget will have limited funds available for group travel. When a performing group is active in competitions, festivals, and community performances, the boosters will often be called upon to budget for travel expenses above those covered by the school.

Office and administration. A school budget should cover basic operational expenses for the music department. However, when the boosters have activities that generate the need for additional office supplies, their budget should cover the additional expenses. Examples might include stationery and postage; newsletter, programs, and printing; installation of telephone line and monthly bills; a telephone answering machine; personal computer, printer, and accessories.

BUDGET DEVELOPMENT

The director should submit his or her assessment of the items needed and the approximate costs to the budget committee. This list will include items that have been submitted on school budget requests and been denied and items that there is simply no chance the administration will approve. They should be placed in order of priority. (Again, be careful not to permit the school administration to abdicate financial support of the program.) Throughout the budgeting process, keep in mind the booster organization's potential to receive free services. Within its ranks you may find printers, painters, carpenters, tailors, publishers, typists, photographers, and musicians. There may also be people in your community who are willing to donate supplies or services.

The budget is developed jointly by the budget and ways and means committees, then approved by the boosters' executive board and full membership. The budget committee prepares the budget. After considering potential for support from the school, the committee decides on each item requested. (See the accompanying figure.) Using the program schedule, the committee then develops a list of estimated expenses for each item

	Director's Need List	
Item	*Estimated Cost*	*Disposition*
Yard Markers	$50.00	Budget (equipment)
Rehearsal Tower	200.00	Budget (construction)
Fender-Rhodes Piano	1,000.00	Defer *
Electric Typewriter	250.00	School
Small Copy Machine	300.00	Repair (school)
Bass Clarinet	1,200.00	Defer**
Office Supplies	300.00	Budget (operating) #
Music Supplies	300.00	Budget (operating) #
Clinicians:		
Flags & Rifles	500.00	Budget (clinicians)
Drill Team	600.00	Budget (clinicians)
Band	1400.00	Budget (clinicians)
Music Arrangements	1,000.00	Budget (operating) #
Field Commander Uniform	225.00	Budget (uniform maintenance)

Notes:
*Request in school budget for next year.
**Request in school budget for next year. If rejected, boosters will include required amount in follow-

Proposed Budget			
Income		*Expense*	
Marching Contest	$1,500	Camp Staff	$1,200
Auction Concession	1,800	Uniform Fund	3,300
Tag Day	2,500	Construction	400
Christmas Sale	2,500	Equipment	1,000
Dances (2)	750	Operating: Boosters	1,000
Pro Football Raffle	1,000	Band	1,000
Spaghetti Dinner	800	Awards	200
Band Appreciation Dinner	500	Transportation	2,000
Concession Stand	4,800	Clinicians	2,500
Registration/Uniform Rental	3,500	Banquet	250
Student Account Donations	250	Festivals	300
TOTAL	$19,900	Film & Pictures	500
		Hospitality	150
		Trips	3,000
		Uniforms Maintenance	1,750
		TOTAL	$18,550

and a schedule of expenditures (cash flow, prepared on a monthly requirement basis) for submission to the ways and means committee.

The ways and means committee evaluates the organization's fundraising potential and schedules and manages fundraising projects. This includes coordinating the fundraising schedule with the music program schedule. The committee discusses methods for providing the financial resources, then develops a schedule for fundraising activities that meets the cash flow requirements and submits a list of the proposed income sources to the budget committee. The budget committee prepares the final proposed budget (see the accompanying figure.)

The final proposed budget is reviewed by the boosters' executive board, which can then discuss each line item. After the executive board has completed its review, it should make a recommendation to the membership for approval.

The budget committee presents the proposed budget to the general membership along with recommendations of the executive board. The ways and means committee presents its plan for fundraising. After discussion, the membership votes on the proposed budget. At subsequent meetings, the budget committee should update the status of the budget and, if appropriate, make recommendations for changes.

After the budget is approved by the membership, develop a combined schedule showing the music program and booster activities. Distribute this schedule to all members of the boosters and to the school administration.

5
Fundraising

A primary function of a booster group is often fundraising. But before starting on fundraising projects, boosters and the music director should be familiar with the school's fundraising policies. Also, keep in mind that going to the public with an open hand too many times can lose their support.

STUDENT PARTICIPATION

Student participation in fundraising activities may be vital to their success. Their enthusiasm and the hours they put in selling candy, manning booths, or washing cars may be indispensable. But care must be taken in enlisting their aid. Don't involve them in so many fundraising activities that their school work could suffer—in fact, be careful that you don't give even the appearance of doing this. Find out if the school district limits the number of hours that students may work or the number of projects they may be involved in.

Trips are by far the most motivating reasons for working on a fundraiser. Many clubs set quotas (either a cash amount or number of units sold) for students to earn their rights to go on a trip without paying an additional fee. But, again, tread lightly. Working on fundraising projects should never be a prerequisite to being in the band or chorus.

ADVANCE PLANNING

A good place to start a fundraising program is by establishing specific goals, both in terms of a specific purchase and the money necessary. Boosters, students, businesses, and the community will respond more readily if they are aware of the goals.

The ways and means committee should begin planning for fundraising events at least six months in advance. This will ensure adequate time to determine areas of responsibility, support requirements, committee assignments, and publicity needs. A six-month lead time also minimizes the danger of overlooking details, a common mistake in a volunteer organization. Too many fundraisers fail because of a detail someone forgot.

The obvious reaction to the six-month lead time is, "We're too busy working on next week's project to worry about next year's project." But leadership can make it become the standard. In the long run, more time will be available, and year-to-year program development will be more successful.

CHOOSING A PROJECT

Seek the advice of parents in the booster group who have sales experience. They can be helpful in planning and executing the fundraising program. A fundraiser in which volunteers provide a service (such as a car wash or flea market) usually involves little or no overhead. Most of what is taken in is profit. The resale of items purchased from a fundraising company, on the other hand, involves accurate planning and sometimes calls for a large cash outlay at the beginning.

If the organization decides to sell a product, check into several suppliers before making a commitment. They will vary in price and support available. Avoid doing business with any supplier that does not address all of the areas below and provide written policy statements at the outset.

Find out about a company's policy on product deliveries and return of unsold merchandise. Also ask about prepayment discounts, volume discounts, incentives such as prizes or bonuses, and any other special arrangements a company may offer. Find whether they make sales kits or publicity material available.

Do check with others who have dealt with a potential supplier before making a commitment. Obtain a list of groups who have bought a given product from a given supplier and contact them. Also contact the Better Business Bureau and other such agencies to obtain information regarding financial stability, reliability, and reputation.

PROJECT EXECUTION

Much of the work on a project can be handled by committees, but there should be one person in charge of running the entire project and keeping appropriate records. This person advises committee chairs and assists in decision making.

A permanent record of each project should be developed that includes the following information:

- Financial goal and results
- Number of participants and total work-hours expended
- Breakdown of areas of responsibility
- Support requirements
- Committee assignments
- Problems encountered
- Recommendations for improvement

Each project can be broken down into specific components. For example, organizing a bazaar might include finance, decorations, publicity, booths, pricing, food preparation and serving, tickets, and cleanup. Establish committees to carry out the project and divide the work load into manageable tasks.

Identify items and services needed to support the project and incorporate them into committee assignments. In the example of the bazaar, the support requirements would include storage space, booths or tables, chairs, signs, price tags, cash boxes, worker identification (such as uniforms, hats, or arm bands), first aid provisions, parking, checkrooms, rest rooms, and security.

Establish a calendar to help each committee meet its objectives. Include milestone dates to measure progress. For example, the publicity committee should have the first drafts of media releases prepared at least two months in advance to allow for approval, revisions, and timely distribution. Coordinate fundraising times and projects with other groups in the school and with local merchants.

Publicize goals and objectives and let the community know about fundraising projects. Make sure that participants generate enthusiasm for the project, the booster organization, and music programs in general.

MARKETING

Good marketing is essential to a successful sale. The product should be something that people normally use. It must also have a fair and reasonable price.

Profit margin. The difference between the price that an organization pays for each item and what it charges for the item is called the markup. The markup divided by the total selling price is the profit margin. For example, if you pay $.75 for an item and sell it for $1.00, the markup is $.25. Divide that by the selling price, and the profit margin is 25 percent. Generally speaking, sales programs in which the markup is less than 33 percent usually fall short of their goals; those that exceed 50 percent are probably overpricing the product and will lose sales.

Don't give the appearance of gouging or taking advantage of customers. Remember, boosters are not looking for donations, but are selling a product. If the cost of a product plus a reasonable markup makes the selling price unreasonable, the project should be rejected.

Calculating profits. In making this calculation, the overall profit is an important consideration.

If sales quotas are used, try the following method to determine them: Subtract the cost from the selling price to get profit per unit. Divide the profit into the fundraising goal to get the minimum number of units that must be sold. Divide that number by the number of members participating in the sale to get the quota for each. Here is an example in which the goal is $3,000, the cost of each item is $1, the selling price is $2, and two hundred people have agreed to help sell the product.

Selling price - Cost = Profit
($2 - $1 = $1)
Goal/profit = Minimum units
($3,000/$1 = 3,000)
Minimum units/participants = Sales quota for each participant
(3,000/200 = 15 per person)

A good average quota is fourteen units per person per project. Statistics show that fundraisers directly associated with a special project (such as a trip) will yield higher sales per participant, around twenty units. Projects for the music program in general yield average sales of from eight to ten units per person.

Project duration. A short-term, "blitz" approach is often effective. The area to be covered is mapped out and sellers are given specific area assignments to avoid duplication and ensure total coverage. It is also helpful to have area chairpersons to whom sellers report. An entire project can be completed in three days or less. For some projects, however, a long-term approach will be more successful. Once the organization establishes a project and repeats it regularly, the community will be aware of its efforts and the quality of the product or service. Examples of long-term projects are concession stand sales at sporting or other recurring events, periodic hoagie sales, and sales of gift wrapping in malls or stores during the holiday season.

SUGGESTIONS

Below is a collection of ideas that have proven successful for many fundraising groups. For events that will draw large crowds, don't forget to provide parking, checkrooms, rest rooms, and picnic tables or other eating areas.

Entertainment, including:
- Films (comedies, classics, features, educational films, student-made videos, travel, art, and music films)
- Music (jazz, classical, and pops events; soloists, folksinging, and marching competitions)
- Dances
- Shows (musical comedies, comedies, follies, serious plays, circus, puppets, minstrel shows, and talent nights)
- Speakers (entertainers, commentators, government leaders, educators, authors, or local celebrities)
- Demonstrations (cooking, crafts, and art)

Recreation and sports, including:
- Exhibition games, invitational tournaments, clinics, lesson series, horse shows or races
- Golf, tennis, table tennis, bowling, card games, checkers, swimming, boxing, wrestling, squash, skating, hockey, polo, baseball, softball, riding, backgammon, and bingo

Bazaars, fairs, and festivals, with:
- Amusements (game booths, strolling musicians, fortune-tellers, races, movies and videos, hobby and handicraft exhibits, pet shows)
- Entertainment (games, puppets, musicians, magicians, clowns, jugglers, or acrobats)
- Demonstrations (jewelry making, gift wrapping, flower arranging, sketching and drawing, and needlework)
- Booths (art, sketches, caricatures, drawings, handicrafts, fresh produce, books, records, country store sales, and items the booster group sells throughout the year)
- Exhibits (paintings, drawings, sculpture, graphics, photography, architecture, city planning, design, needlework, health, science, conservation, history, sports, recreation, antiques, livestock, and crops)
- Food (drinks, meals, snacks, and desserts)
- Sales (party supplies, accessories, local items, candles, toys, bird houses, bird feeders, garden tools, decorated shopping bags, souvenir items, jewelry, gift wrap, dried/artificial flowers, and craft kits)

Parties with various themes, such as:
- Game parties (bridge, canasta, pinochle, checkers, and chess)
- Dances
- Outings (bus tours, restaurant dinners, riverboat rides, out-of-town shopping sprees)
- Miscellaneous (scavenger hunts, treasure hunts, and car rallies)

Tours of local gardens or houses, concentrating on architecture, remodeling, furnishings, special rooms, patios or decks, landscaping, art collections, and libraries

Fashion shows:
- Based on special themes (back to school, vacation time, play time, history, international or seasonal fashions; new fabrics, colors, or designers; or titles of books, songs, movies, and plays)
- Based on types of clothing (resort wear, lounge wear, party clothes, bridal fashions, sportswear, seasonal styles, separates, or children's wear)

Meals for a crowd, such as:

- Picnics, barbecues, open houses, teas, coffees, brunches, breakfasts, luncheons, dinners, suppers, receptions, banquets, desserts, progressive dinners, and dinner dances
- Meals based on themes such as current events, politics, holidays, celebrations, history, and music
- Meals with different serving styles (sit-down, walk-away, picnic, formal, cafeteria, family–style)

Sales of products such as:
- New items (gifts, cosmetics, local products, stationery, china, handmade items, boutique items, candles, bulbs, plants, calendars, cookbooks, jewelry, fruit, kits, jokes and gimmick items, and souvenir items)
- Used or recycled items (clothing, furniture, toys, sports equipment, baby items, appliances, antiques, costumes, china, glassware, bric-a-brac)
- Items sold at auctions, consignment sales, rummage sales, consignment shops, thrift shops, flea markets, bazaars, fairs, door-to-door, and those sold by phone or mail order

Services such as car washes, newspaper drives, recycling of bottles and aluminum cans, taking inventory for local stores, and performing yard work

6

Travel

Taking a trip with a music group is one of the most exciting experiences that many students have in school. But it should be more than just a source of motivation; the learning value should be clear. The trip should include musical performances, historical and cultural enrichment, and personal development through the acceptance of individual responsibilities without dependence on direct and continual parental supervision.

Trips should be put together with care. A disappointing experience can mean loss of support from the school administration, students, and parents.

INITIAL PLANNING

Before you get started, consider whether you have enough lead time to organize the trip you have in mind. Is there time to get the school's permission, get on family calendars, raise funds, make arrangements, and learn the music? If you have any doubts, aim for another time.

The trip coordinator should assist the director in the initial planning so that he or she will have the basic understandings on which specific plans and arrangements will be based later.

Sit down with the principal and explain the trip you have in mind. Be prepared to supply the following information:

- The type of musical performance—such as contest, festival, exchange, clinic, parade, workshop, or community event
- Length of the trip
- Estimated costs for housing, meals, transportation, attractions, and so forth
- Activities planned in addition to the music performances

A BRIEF ITINERARY

When you talk with your principal, discuss policies on the amount of time students can spend out of classes and liability. Also, be sure you understand your school's policy regarding trip approval so you can obtain all the necessary information and allow sufficient time for processing your request. For example, a principal may have the authority to approve a trip of less than three days within the state, while a longer trip may have to be submitted to the school board for authority. In the first case a decision would be expected in a few days, while in the second you might have to wait several weeks.

CHOOSING A TRAVEL AGENT

When planning a trip lasting several days or covering several hundred miles, consider using a travel agent. Travel agents are paid by the transportation companies and hotels to provide services such as information, reservations, and ticketing. The agent's service should be available at no charge to you and may save you some money. Special consideration should be given to travel agents who deal primarily with music groups since they have specialized information others may not be able to provide (about such things as security of instruments and equipment and festivals, competitions, concerts, and other performance activities).

Find out if the agency you are considering is approved by the Airlines Reporting Corporation, 1709 New York Avenue NW, Washington, DC 20006, and the International Air Transport Association, 1730 K Street NW, Washington, DC 20006, (the domestic and international airline accreditation bodies). Find out how much liability insurance the travel agency carries. The agent should be willing to give you a copy of the policy or a certificate of insurance.

Check the travel agent's references through such sources as the bank, the local chamber of commerce, and the Better Business Bureau. Request a list of groups the agent has handled, and contact a few for evaluations.

WORKING TOGETHER

Once you decide on a travel agent, the responsibility for the success of the trip is shared by the agent, the booster organization, and you. The following items should be covered by the travel agent, but it's a good idea to specify how you want them handled.

Contract. Request a written contract that spells out each party's responsibilities as well as payment schedules and cancellation penalties. The contract should be approved by the music director, the principal, and at least three persons in positions of authority within the booster organization. You may want the entire executive committee to approve any contract or written agreement.

Confirmations. Insist that all confirmations for travel, lodging, group meals, concerts, and any other planned group functions be in writing. Do not accept telephone confirmations.

Spot checks. Check up on some of the suppliers that will provide for your trip, such as hotels, restaurants, concert sites, and coaches. Be sure the travel agent has information on liability insurance, locations of restaurants and hotels, and classes of accommodations for which you are booked.

Personal contact. Request a visit from the travel agent or the agent's representative to talk with you and the booster organization. Be prepared to ask questions. For international travel, insist that a responsible, experienced member of the travel agency staff travel with your group. For domestic travel, request that a representative assist you at least when you are at your principal destination.

TRAVEL

Transportation decisions need to be made carefully. Buses are normally more economical than other carriers. Air travel provides considerable time savings but must be supplemented by ground transportation at the destination. On long trips, bus travel can reduce lodging costs by scheduling departure times to provide for overnight travel; the bus replaces the motel for one night each way.

Bus travel. If you elect to travel by bus, obtain price quotes from two or more competing bus companies. Determine each company's policy for repair or replacement of buses en route. Major companies can provide replacement buses with a minimum of lost time. Smaller or independent companies may be at the mercy of local repair shops when breakdowns occur. Once you have selected the bus company, be sure to obtain the location and timing of stops for driver changes and refueling. Also, visit the garage to examine and approve the type of bus you will be using.

Air travel. Air travel requires close coordination of arrangements for transportation to and from the airport, check in, and baggage and equipment handling. Airlines will assist you with these arrangements. When using a charter flight you can usually arrange to have equipment, baggage, and passengers loaded directly on and off the aircraft, bypassing the normal procedures. When traveling on regularly scheduled flights, you can arrange for some airlines to tag your luggage and equipment for direct loading. Special boarding and check in arrangements are also possible.

LODGING

Your selection of a place to stay should be based on considerations of cost, quality, location (both the immediate environment and proximity to sites of scheduled activities), and policies regarding youth groups.

Rates. Obtain costs for quadruple, triple, double, and single occupancy. Determine the policy on complimentary rooms. Establish deposit and payment requirements, check in and check out times, and the availability of secure storage areas for instruments and equipment. Economy motels that do not have lounges, clubs, and expensive restaurants often provide acceptable facilities and usually have better rates.

Quality of the facilities at a given site can be verified a number of ways, but firsthand knowledge obtained through actual visits is the best. Several travel publications rate the quality of lodging accommodations. Travel agents will be able to find this information for you.

Location is a very important consideration. Cost is affected by location; motels on the fringes of cities are normally cheaper. The distance between your quarters and activity sites will influence your travel schedule. Be sure that the location minimizes risk to the students.

MEALS

Plan sit-down or buffet meals in advance, and call the restaurant so that they'll have sufficient help. You need not, however, schedule all meals at restaurants. Meal variations might include a pool-side barbecue, pizza party, or picnic at a roadside rest stop or park. Schedule independent lunches when time permits.

Keep meals on schedule; they should not take time away from other events. For bus trips, have students plan ahead and organize coolers for the bus.

CHAPERONS

Chaperons can be a major factor in a trip's success. The ratio should be one chaperon to every ten to fifteen students (this does not include the director's staff). Appoint a chief or head chaperon as the main liaison between the director and the other chaperons.

Hold a meeting with all chaperons and staff prior to departure to familiarize them with the schedule, rules, regulations, and policies. Should schedule changes become necessary after the trip is in progress, notify chaperons promptly, preferably before advising the students.

Provide name tags to be worn by all staff and chaperons. This is important for both students and outsiders who may need to have contact with your group. Develop a schedule that will provide the chaperons with specific duties, special requirements, and any planned free time.

HEALTH FORMS

Obtain a health form that provides pertinent information for emergency treatment of every person on the trip—adults as well as students. (See the accompanying suggested form.) These forms should be kept with the group at all times. Note, however, the paragraph on the form explaining the limitations of parental consent. As stated on pages 12–13 of William R. Hazard's *Tort Liability for Music Educators* (Reston, VA: Music Educators National Conference, 1979), "Consent forms only advise parents of planned activities; they do not reduce the duty of care owed to students and they do not waive any liability for negligence."

A person trained in first aid should accompany the group. If a parent is not properly qualified to fill this role, hire a nurse or contact the local rescue squad or hospital for assistance. See the accompanying list for suggested contents of a first aid kit.

RULES AND DISCIPLINE

Provide students with written rules and regulations that establish the standards of conduct for the trip. The director, with input from the students, school administration, and parents, should determine the policies to be enforced. Students and parents will understand and respect rules and regulations when they have had some input into their development.

Regulations are of no value to you or the students unless there are disciplinary actions established for them. There should be different levels of discipline set in advance so that students and parents will know the consequences for certain actions. Some disciplinary actions will reflect school policy; others should be developed by the director. In addition to general policies that apply to all situations, there should be special guides that apply to specific situations such as behavior and attire for a beach or theme park. The following items should be addressed:

Travel behavior. Specify things such as use of seat belts, amount of movement throughout the carrier, group courtesy (particularly during overnight travel), littering, and safety regulations.

Smoking. If permitted, specify where, when, and in what attire smoking is allowed. Refer to school policy.

Use of alcohol and illegal drugs. Refer to school policy.

Coeducational visits. If allowed, specify times and policies. It is a common practice to state that when boys and girls visit in each others' rooms, the door must remain open.

Curfews. These should be specified in the schedule and strictly enforced.

Uniform and equipment standards. Define clearly. Appearance will have an influence on performances as well as the impression made on others.

Tardiness. Don't allow a few students to delay the schedule and inconvenience the whole group.

Dress code for group activities. Define "casual dress" when called for in the schedule.

SCHEDULING

Scheduling is as important as any task in the planning and execution of a trip. Necessary details include date, day of the week, time, event or activity, attire, and duration for each activity on the schedule. Once a schedule is finalized, distribute copies to

MEDICAL INFORMATION AND RELEASE FORM

_____
Name of Program

Student's Name_____
                last   first   middle

Sex_____ Date of Birth_____/_____/_____
                     Month   Day   Year

Name of Parent/Guardian_____

Home Phone _____

Home Address_____
Business Phones_____/_____
                          Father   Mother

Emergency
Contact_____
        Name   Address   Phone

Does student have school insurance?   Yes_____   No_____
Type_____

Parent/Guardian
Insurance Company
Name_____   Policy
Number _____
Military Dependent? Yes _____   No_____
Military I.D. Number_____

Indicate any problems you now have or have had with the following: (Use back of this form for explanations.)

_____Epilepsy	_____Rheumatic Fever	_____Heart Palpitations
_____Dizziness, Fainting	_____Kidney, Urinary	_____Frequent Colds
_____Ear, Eye, Nose, Throat	_____Asthma, Bronchitis	_____Hay Fever
_____Stomach Trouble	_____Jaundice, Hepatitis	_____Diabetes
_____Bee Sting Allergy	_____Food Allergies*	_____Medication Allergies*

*Specify
allergies_____
If you are currently taking any medication, please indicate here_____

Family Physician_____
Phone_____

Alternate
Physician_____
Phone_____

NOTICE: By law, a parent cannot consent in advance to any and all manners of emergency care. It is understandable that in cases other than the need for immediate emergency treatment, the attending physician may defer treatment pending the parent's express permission to administer specific professional services.

IN AN EMERGENCY, THE SCHOOL HAS MY PERMISSION TO CALL MY FAMILY PHYSICIAN, OR ANOTHER PHYSICIAN IF MY FAMILY PHYSICIAN OR I CANNOT BE CONTACTED.

Signature of
Parent/Guardian_____Date_____

ALL INFORMATION PROVIDED WILL BE TREATED AS CONFIDENTIAL

FIRST AID KIT

Instruments
  Scissors: bandage type with blunt ends preferred to protect against cutting skin
  Tweezers: pointed, straight, or angled tips; or scissors type
  Fingernail and toenail clippers
  Safety razor: double-edge, and extra blades
  Single-edge razor blades

Bandages
  Bandages: variety of sizes—1/2", 1", 3", 4", 6"
  Gauze: several rolls, cling type preferred
  Adhesive tape: variety of widths—1/2", 1", 2"; store in plastic bags
  Sling: triangular, approximately 6" x 4" x 1"; purchase in small container
  Ace bandages: variety of sizes—3", 4", 6"
  ABD pads: 5" x 9"; excellent for compression and covering large wounds
  Eye patches: individually wrapped

Splints
  Short arm and long arm: four of each
  OCL: 2" or 3" width; obtain from local emergency department, orthopedist, or doctor.

Medications
  Prescription drugs: Have students turn over any prescription medications to person in charge and dispense according to doctor's directions.
  Over-the-counter drugs: Including aspirin, acetaminophen, antihistamines, decongestants, cough preparations, skin preparations, and so forth.
  NOTE: Over-the-counter drugs carry fewer problems with liability, but those dispensing them must receive permission to do so.

Other items
  Ammonia inhalants
  Tongue depressors
  Long cotton applicators or standard cotton swabs
  Dial or Ivory soap: small sample sizes individually wrapped; use for washing wounds (cuts or abrasions)
  Antiseptics: hydrogen peroxide or betadine
  NOTE: Do not include iodine, Mercurochrome, or Merthiolate.
  Ice bags: chemical-filled bag or container that can be filled with ice
  Safety pins
  Airways: small, medium, large with instructions on how to insert (obtain from local hospital or rescue squad)
  Emesis basin: plastic or other
  First aid booklet (be sure it is up-to-date)
  A large standard metal tool box with a lift-out tray is needed to carry all the supplies listed above. In addition, a large plastic or cloth bag that closes with a drawstring is recommended. Individual items should be stored in small metal or plastic containers, or plastic bags.

the administration, parents, and students. When the trip starts, provide copies to the drivers, chaperons, tour guides, hotels, and any others who will be associated with the trip (such as those providing meals, entertainment, or other services).

Decide who will make changes and how the changes will be announced so that "rumor" changes can be minimized. Good times to announce schedule changes are at sit-down meals, on buses, and at room checks. In preparing the schedule, consider the following:

Activity time. Allow the proper portion of time to each event. A roadside stop should last only twenty to thirty minutes, while a theme park visit will be eight to ten hours.

Preparation time. Allow ample time for such activities as loading and unloading, attendance checks, travel, meals, and so on, based on the size of the group.

Rest time. Plan activities carefully around major events. Do not schedule exhausting activities on the day of an important performance.

ROOMING AND SEATING LISTS

Establishing rooming and transportation lists in advance will simplify boarding and attendance checks. Allowing students to sign up for travel and rooming companions will generally contribute to the harmonious atmosphere that is desirable for all trips. Provide the lists to all staff and chaperons. Furnish the hotel with your rooming lists and the preferred location of chaperon and staff rooms in relation to the students' rooms.

EMERGENCY CONTACTS

Identify at least two booster parents as emergency contacts, preferably ones who can be reached at home while the students are on the trip. These parents should attend all preliminary chaperon meetings. Provide them with phone numbers where you can be contacted throughout the trip. Give their names and phone numbers to the students' parents. This function can be handled by the telephone committee.

TRIP PAYMENTS

After determining the costs of a trip, prepare a permission/obligation form to establish individual commitments to the trip. The form should be signed by the parents and the student and returned to the director. An example is as follows:

> "I/we give permission for [student's name] to go with the [name of organization] to [trip location]. We understand that the total student cost is ($xx.xx) and that payment in full is to be made by [date]. In the event that [student's name] is withdrawn from the trip by us, we understand that all monies not recoverable by the [name of your organization] will be owed by us and are not refundable."

This will provide the information necessary to make commitments on transportation, reservations, and services required for the trip. An information sheet should accompany this form providing a breakdown of all items and activities covered by the students' cost, and identifying those extras for which the student will be responsible. The information sheet should also inform the students and their parents of any known risks connected with the event and travel. For more information on this subject, see page twelve of William R. Hazard's *Tort Liability and the Music Educator* (Reston, VA: Music Educators National Conference, 1979). It is also advisable to set up an incremental payment schedule so that the entire amount is not due at one time. This will generate the funds necessary to cover any required deposits.

PUBLICITY

Do not overlook the importance of publicizing the trip. As soon as possible after finalizing your itinerary, the publicity committee should prepare releases to the local media. These releases should include information on the dates, activities, destinations, and any fundraising activities that will help pay for the trip. (See the next chapter, "Publicity," for a sample adapted from the Music in Our Schools Month resource booklet, published by MENC). The frequency and newsworthiness of the releases should build as the departure date nears.

The boosters should remember to be positive and not apologetic for calling upon the community for support. The amount of community support gained will accrue in direct proportion to how well the community has been informed. Provide follow-up releases after the trip acknowledging the accomplishments of the group and contributions of community members.

7
Publicity

Publicity can make a world of difference in fundraising and music advocacy efforts. When a bond issue comes up or the school board is deciding budget priorities, it's nice to know that the voters in the community are aware of—and take pride in—the music programs. And when a specific fundraising event comes up, it's nice to know that everybody in the community has had at least one opportunity to read or hear about it.

There isn't much mystery to getting media publicity. It's largely a matter of putting yourself in the place of editors and news programmers. They are looking for timely, well-presented information that will interest their audience. But the simple requirement that your releases be interesting implies hours of work and months of planning. Successful booster organizations maintain ongoing programs for dispensing information to the community that cultivates and stimulates their interest and support. Most of the information in this chapter pertains to publicity through the media. But don't overlook other strategies such as putting up posters or speaking before civic organizations.

REFERENCE LIBRARY

A publicity program is founded on a customized library set up by the boosters' publicity committee. The library contains standard information and visual material for support of publicity releases and presentations.

Music program overview. The publicity committee should develop a summary that describes the entire music program. This description can be handed out any time they need to give someone basic information about the program and can be sent out with press releases. All elements of the program should be listed, including general music courses, large performing groups, and specialized performing groups such as show choirs, Orff ensembles, or chamber groups.

Prepare a standard narrative of all the program's accomplishments. The narrative should include types of activities students participate in through the music program and results of specific events. When possible, include complimentary quotations from prominent people in the community.

Visual resources. The publicity committee should maintain a file of photos, color slides, and videocassettes. This section of the publicity library should cover performances, rehearsals, sectionals, fundraising events, and booster functions (meetings and support activities).

Newspaper editors prefer black-and-white photographs and usually request 5" x 7" prints. This size provides them with good reproduction quality and allows flexibility in cropping. Prints can be filed by subject. Note the negative number on the back of each picture to assist in retrieving negatives when additional prints are required. Create an index of all prints, listing them by subject and negative number.

Color slides are valuable for group presentations and for releases to television. Slides can be filed in clear pages and stored in a three-ring binder. Use the same index system for slides as for prints, and have duplicate slides prepared in advance.

Videocassettes are effective for presentations to civic organizations and for recruitment activities. (They are also being requested more frequently to accompany applications to participate in special events.)

PUBLICITY CAMPAIGN

The success of a publicity campaign depends on proper timing. Before the start of a school year, the publicity committee should review the goals, activities, and schedule of the music program and of the boosters. They should prepare an initial media release, giving an overview of the year's activities to develop interest in the program.

Each major activity of the music department and all support efforts of the boosters should be covered by publicity releases. Before each event, write a release that covers the preparations. Write follow-up releases that state the results in a positive way. These are most important for sustaining interest in the program. Don't forget to insert notices in the "coming events" sections of local papers and newsletters.

The most efficient way to reach a large audience is through newspapers, magazines, radio, and television. List all media sources available in the area. Keep a record of individual contacts, phone numbers, and mailing addresses for each. For further information, see the MENC publication, *Beyond the Classroom: Informing Others*, which contains many suggestions for communicating with the media.

PREPARATION OF MATERIALS

The following guidelines will help the publicity committee establish a good working relationship with the media:

Submit clean, concise articles supported by appropriate visual material. If you ask a news photographer to photograph an event, determine when the pictures can be taken (prior to, during, or following the event). Don't expect the photographer to wait through a long business meeting only to shoot three or four pictures of your officers afterwards. It is better to have someone in your group take pictures and submit the best with your copy.

Learn what is considered news, what is expected of a news source, and how to write news stories. A well-written news story is concise and contains useful information. A good article gets to the point quickly and doesn't waste words. There are two basic story forms: the straight news story, which consists of events that have occurred or are about to occur; and the feature story, comprising ideas, discussions, interpretations, background, or human interest matters.

For a straight news story about an event that has occurred or is anticipated, use short, uncomplicated sentences. Be especially aware of the need for objectivity, accuracy, and brevity. The most important element of the straight news story is the lead, or opening. It may be as short as one sentence, or as long as a paragraph. It is a summary of the important facts and answers the primary questions the reader will ask: what, where, when, who, how, and why.

A feature article might be about an unusually successful student, a performing group, an interesting activity in a general music class, the experience of going to band camp, or anything else that can be spun into an interesting story. Feature stories are usually not dependent upon spot news developments. For this reason, it is possible to hold them for publication as long as the content of the article remains accurate and timely.

Whichever type of article seems most appropriate, think about who the readers are. Be concise. Omit details that are not pertinent to the subject. Keep paragraphs short, building each around a main topic. Write in the present tense. Check all names, dates, places, and other facts for accuracy. Give complete dates (Wednesday, October 10) instead of using terms like "tomorrow" or "next Wednesday."

Find out when publication deadlines are, and meet them. All news copy should be typewritten, double-spaced, on one side of the page only. Text should begin two to three inches down from the top. Never put more than one story on a sheet of paper even if the story is only one paragraph long. See the accompanying news release for a sample.

A publicity committee member's name and telephone number should go in the upper right corner of the first page. Just beneath, include a few words indicating the subject matter covered in the story. If the date of publication is important, type "For release..." and the date of release. Otherwise, type "For immediate release."

If the story runs more than one page, center the word "more" at the bottom of the first page and continue about two inches down from the top of the second page. In the upper left corner of the second page, write "Page 2: Booster Meeting." At the close of the story, type "# # #", "-30-", or the word "end" centered below the final paragraph.

News Release

For release: [date]   Contact: [name]
Chairperson
Music in Our Schools Month
[address]
[phone number]

LOCAL SCHOOL PERFORMS CONCERT

The [name] school will give a free concert on [day of the week], [date], at [time] in the school auditorium.
[name of director], a music educator at [school], will conduct the [band, chorus, orchestra] in the performance, which will feature both popular and traditional selections.
The concert is part of the thirteenth national observance of Music in our Schools Month, which is held during March. This year's theme is "_____."
Music in our Schools Month is sponsored by MENC: The National Association for Music Education, a 70,000–member professional association.
For more information about the concert, call [name and phone].

#   #   #

8
Communications

The success of a volunteer organization depends on the participation, interest, and enthusiasm it generates. Regular communication is a key to this, and a newsletter is one of the most effective ways of doing it. A newsletter keeps less active members informed, provides public acknowledgement of the efforts of active members, and maintains interest between meetings or projects. It can be as simple as a single typewritten sheet, or several pages printed with a desktop publishing program.

NEWSLETTER

Organization and Schedule. An editor or chairperson should be named to be in charge of the newsletter. This person should be a member of the boosters' executive board and knowledgeable about the activities of the organization. The editor should select an assistant or co-chairperson.

A regular publication schedule is generally more desirable than publishing on an "as needed" basis. Most newsletters are published monthly or bimonthly; some are published ten or eleven times a year (omitting July and/or December). An August issue permits timely coverage of activities, such as band or music camp and uniform distribution, that occur prior to the start of the school year.).

The editor should decide the date he or she would like each issue to be in the hands of readers, then work backward from that date to determine deadlines for delivery to the post office, delivery to and from the printer, completion of the camera-ready copy, and finally for submission of items to the editorial staff.

Content. Production of a newsletter can be viewed as having four basic steps: writing, typesetting, printing, and distributing. Here are some suggestions for the written content of the newsletter.

Incorporate a wide variety of information from many sources. This can include regular columns by important booster representatives, lists or descriptions of upcoming events, feature articles contributed by booster or faculty members, or even letters to the editor.

The booster chapter president should have a regular column in the newsletter to highlight current events or upcoming activities, express appreciation, or report on recent decisions or achievements. The president's message should not deal with issues that are school-oriented except to offer reinforcement to a topic addressed by the music director, when appropriate.

The music director should also have a regular column to discuss the music program and goals, school policies, student preparation, upcoming musical events, and the importance of the booster support.

Executive Board members and chairs of standing or temporary committees should provide reports when appropriate. The "trio approach" is often very effective. This involves a minimum of three reports on a particular activity at different times. The first report covers planning, preparations, and a general description of what is to be accomplished. The second, published just prior to the date when the event is to take place, identifies those who are assisting, gives schedule details, and reinforces the importance of the event to the support of the music program. The final report recognizes those who contributed to the success of the event.

Students in the music program, such as student directors and section leaders, can contribute reports on their activities, goals, and accomplishments.

A block calendar of the school year should be printed in the first issue of the newsletter each year. It may have notations for school and community events in addition to booster and music department events. In addition, a monthly listing of upcoming events should be in each issue. It should include times, locations, and the names and phone numbers of contact persons.

Format. The newsletter should be quickly identifiable as part of the booster organization or program. Using a logo, mascot, or clever title is the best way to accomplish this recognition.

The arrangement and composition of a newsletter should follow the same general plan for each issue (except in the event of a special issue). This helps the readers know what to expect, and it helps the editor assemble each issue and plan several months ahead.

The most common method of numbering newsletters is by volume and number. "Volume" indicates the year of publication, and "number" indicates which issue of that year. The first issue would be "Volume 1, number 1," followed by "Volume 1, number 2." The first issue of the second year would be "Volume 2, number 1," and so on. This information, along with the title, month and year of publication, and name of the booster group is usually part of the standard heading used for each issue.

Typesetting can mean typing a neat copy on a typewriter or word processor, producing a copy with a desktop publishing software package, or actually having the newsletter professionally typeset. Printing can mean mimeographing, photocopying, or offset printing. The methods the newsletter committee chooses will depend on equipment and money available.

Distribution. Send the newsletter to anyone in the community who may be interested in helping support the music program and anyone who may have an influence on decision makers in the district, county, or state. These may include:

- Parents of all students in the music program
- Parents of former students still in the community
- Parents of students in other district school music programs
- School faculty members and administrators
- School board members
- Local elected and appointed officials

- Local civic organizations
- Local businesses, merchants, and suppliers, especially those with whom your program does business

The best way to deliver newsletters is by mail. (The worst way is to send them home with students.) Different postal rates may apply, depending on the status of the booster organization. If the school accepts the newsletter as a school publication, the booster organization may be able to mail it using the school's nonprofit public institution bulk rate. If the booster organization has established nonprofit status through the Internal Revenue Service, it qualifies for the nonprofit bulk rate. If the organization doesn't qualify for the nonprofit rate, regular bulk rate is still less expensive than first class mail. There is a fee for the privilege of using bulk rate and a required minimum number of pieces per mailing. The local post office can supply details and requirements.

TELEPHONE COMMITTEE

The telephone committee provides rapid, accurate, and effective internal communications through a telephone tree. Its primary mission is to supplement the newsletter and meetings as a means of communication. It takes on special importance when members need to be contacted quickly, though it shouldn't be overused for this. Some uses for the telephone committee include emergency contacts when a group is touring; reminder calls about meetings; verification that the newsletter has been received; and changes in plans for fundraising events.

Organization. The organization of the telephone committee distributes the work load among several members. It is important for this committee to have co-chairpersons instead of a single chair. This provides easier access to the committee and reduces the need for having one person always available to attend to committee functions. The committee is structured in a pyramidal form, so that each member makes six to twelve calls per task. If, for example, two co-chairs each call five committee members, who in turn each call six boosters, a total of seventy-two families can be contacted quickly without the expenditure of too much time by any one individual.

If the booster organization supports more than one performing group, you may want to have more than one telephone tree operated by the telephone committee. Members of the committee should then include chairpersons for each group. A backup system should also be established under which a co-chair can make calls for an absent member.

Calling Lists. Successful operation of the telephone committee requires accurate calling lists. Prepare a general membership calling list, to be maintained by the co-chairpersons, and divide it among the committee members. There may be families who have unlisted phone numbers and prefer to keep them unpublished. Their numbers should not be included on a general membership roster, but they should be made known to the co-chairpersons and to the one committee member to whom they are assigned.

Using the Telephone Tree. Use of the telephone committee should be controlled. Requests should always come from the president, music director, or authorized members of the executive board. When time permits, information to be relayed should be written. Messages should be short, clear, and concise, and should contain sufficient information that lengthy explanations won't be necessary. A deadline by which all calls are to be made (and, if necessary, information relayed back to the chairs) should be included.

Appendix 1
Constitution and Bylaws

A complete, up-to-date, and realistic constitution and bylaws are important for the protection and guidance of a music booster association. They provide a justification of the organization's purposes and methods of operation to your school board, your bank, your members, the Internal Revenue Service, and anyone else who might raise questions. A constitution is a document that records the system of fundamental laws and principles that normally governs the operation of an association. It generally states the organization's name, purpose, and structure.

Bylaws govern the internal affairs of an organization. Generally, they describe how the organization is to be managed and how its purposes are to be achieved. They define the powers, duties, and limitations of officers and committees; and the relations, rights, and duties of members.

Unless you use articles of incorporation there is no fixed form for bylaws. Generally, almost any format and any degree of detail is acceptable as long as the essential elements of purpose and management are clearly defined. The constitution and bylaws presented below present ideas, concepts, and specific wording used by successful booster groups. Items are listed in random order with no attempt to recommend one statement or wording over another. Each booster organization must decide which statements are most appropriate for its purposes.

To create your own constitution and bylaws, read through the list of suggestions and select statements you feel are necessary for efficient management of your organization. If no one statement fits your situation, write your own. If you feel a section is unnecessary, omit it. Bylaws should be complete but concise.

The list of bylaws here is based on one compiled by C. Dean Streator, chairman of the Music Booster Affiliates of the Pennsylvania Music Educators Association. His information was derived from bylaws submitted by twenty booster organizations and the sample bylaws in the *AMBA Management Guide*, which this book replaces.

CONSTITUTION

This sample constitution contains articles defining the name, purpose, and structure of an organization.

Article I: Name

1. The name of the organization, association, or corporation shall be _____.
2. This organization, association, or corporation shall be known as _____.
3. _____ (Hereafter known as the Organization, Association, or Corporation).
4. This organization will include [names of schools] and any other school(s) subsequently built within the school district.
5. The principal office of the corporation shall be at (location) or other such places as the board of directors may from time to time appoint or the activities of the corporation may require.

Article II: Purpose

1. To promote and encourage community/area support of the [school/area] Music Department(s), with the following objectives:
    a. To involve the community in supporting the music department.
    b. To supplement school board support of music activities.
    c. To provide financial support for non-school activities.
    d. To encourage students to participate in the activities of the Music Booster Club.
    e. To encourage music department exposure.
2. To provide financial assistance and services for the music department and to all supportive units as may be added.
3. To aid in the development of student interest.
4. To promote student leadership and responsibility.
5. To arouse and maintain an enthusiastic public interest in all phases of the music department.
6. To cooperate with those in charge of the music department and the school board to the end that the school music department maintain the highest possible degree of efficiency.
7. To bring into closer relationship the home and school, that parents and music departments may cooperate intelligently in all phases of the school's music program.
8. To aid the music program in such manner as members of the association and the music director shall deem fitting and proper.
9. To stimulate student and community interest in appreciation of the school music programs.
10. To promote and encourage student cultural improvement through appreciation of fine music.
11. To actively support all performances of the school music programs.
12. To lend all possible support, both moral and financial, to the general, instrumental, and vocal music programs in the schools.
13. To serve as a means of communication to keep parents of [performing group] members informed as to the activities and projects of the [performing group].
14. To provide for the [performing group] members those things over and above that which is provided by the school board, such as:

a. Extra activities throughout the year
   b. Refreshments
   c. Banquet
   d. Awards, in keeping with school policy and approved by the executive board and music directors
   e. Funds for any projects, activities, or trips that might be proposed and approved
15. To make all plans and carry out fundraising for support of activities and projects.
16. To assume responsibility for publicity covering any activity or project sponsored by the organization.
17. To maintain enthusiastic interest in band, chorus, and orchestra activities in cooperation with the music director, assistants, and the school administration.
18. To work with and assist the music director(s).
19. To aid in the improvement of the general, instrumental, and vocal music program of the school through a better understanding of the goals and the purpose of the band, chorus, and orchestra and to give moral and financial assistance whenever possible.

Article III: Structure

1. Under the provisions specified in the bylaws, this organization shall be governed by the elected officers, the executive committee, and the membership, with the cooperation of the school music director(s).

BYLAWS

These sample bylaws include articles pertaining to membership, officers, committees, meetings, parliamentary procedure, fiscal and financial matters, awards, amendments, and dissolution.

Article I: Membership

1. The association shall have only one class of members. The members shall be all parents of students participating in the organization's activities and any person whose interest is to further the purpose of the organization.
2. The membership of this organization shall include any adult willing to promote the purpose of the organization.
3. Members shall be the parents or legal guardians of the students in the music organizations and any interested persons desiring to participate in the functions of the organization.
4. Student officers of (performing group), which include president, vice-president, secretary, treasurer, and librarian, shall be ex-officio, non-voting members of the organization.
5. Music students may attend meetings as requested by the executive committee.
6. Students are not eligible for membership.
7. Membership shall not be limited.
8. Parents of pupils active in the music department are automatically active members.
9. Alumni of the high school music organizations are automatically members.
10. Other interested parties may become honorary members.
11. Members shall be those persons accepted by a two-thirds vote of the board of directors who assume the rights and duties and accept the objects and purposes of this corporation.

12. The board of directors, by affirmative vote of two-thirds of all the members of the board, may suspend or expel a member for cause after an appropriate hearing, and may, by a majority vote of those present at any regular constituted meeting, terminate the membership of any member who becomes ineligible for membership, or suspend or expel any member who shall be in default in the payment of any dues or assessments.
13. Each member shall have one vote on any matter under consideration by the membership at a meeting of the membership.
14. Membership shall be for a one-year period.
15. Associate membership may be extended to any of those in the community interested in the purpose of the organization; annual dues of [amount] per family. Associate members have all the privileges of regular members except voting and holding office.
16. Members shall not be required to pay a membership fee.

Article II: Officers

General Guidelines
1. The officers of this organization shall be president, vice president, secretary, and treasurer.
2. The officers of this organization shall be president, vice president, secretary, treasurer, adviser, corresponding secretary, elementary coordinator, historian, liaison, librarian, membership chairman, middle school coordinator, music department chairman, parliamentarian, president-elect, publicity director, senior high coordinator, and such other officers and assistant officers as the needs of the corporation may require.
3. Any member of the organization in good standing shall be eligible to serve as an officer.
4. The music director and assistants may participate in an advisory capacity.
5. The music director and assistants shall be ex officio, nonvoting members of the organization.
6. The officers of this organization shall serve without compensation.
7. The vice president will automatically become president the following term.
8. Only one person of any family may hold an elected office during any one school year. However, one family may jointly hold an office.
9. To hold an office, a member must have a child who is currently active in the band or chorus and must be a member in good standing.
10. An officer must be the parent of a student of the music department during his or her entire term of office.
11. No officer shall succeed himself or herself.
12. No member shall serve as an officer for more than two years.
13. No person shall serve more than one term in the same office.
14. Officers may not be elected to more than two successive terms in the same office.
15. A member shall hold only one office at a time.
16. Any number of offices may be held by the same person.
17. Officers of this association shall serve for a term of one year, but may be re-elected.
18. The board of directors may secure the fidelity of any or all such officers by bond or otherwise.

19. The four elected parent officers serve as official parent chaperons for trips; their expenses for these trips shall be paid by the association.
20. All officers shall perform the duties prescribed in the parliamentary authority in addition to those outlined in these bylaws and those assigned from time to time.
21. All officers shall deliver to their successors all official material within 30 days following elections.
22. All officers shall transfer to their successors all books, papers, and other property of the association in their possession after the [month of election] meeting and prior to the [next month] meeting.

Nominations
1. A nominating committee shall be appointed by the president at the general membership meeting in [month].
2. The music director shall also serve on this committee.
3. The committee shall attempt to reach each member to establish their interest in serving.
4. Candidates will be presented at the general membership meeting in [month].
5. The nominating committee must present all names at the [month] meeting with nominations being accepted from the floor, with the consent of the nominee.
6. The committee shall present the slate to the president for presentation to the body at the [month] meeting.
7. Nominations may also be made by members of the organization. Such nominations must be in writing and filed with the secretary no less than five days before the annual meeting at which the officers are elected.
8. The slate shall be given to the president prior to the executive board meeting preceding the final membership meeting of the year at which time the election shall be held.
9. General membership must be notified of the slate in writing at the same time that meeting notification is given.
10. Nominating report to be given and voted upon at the [month] meeting.
11. Election of officers will take place at the [month] meeting and the officers will assume their duties on [date].
12. The nominating committee shall follow the accepted procedure of offering the office of president to the current vice president if they deem him or her to be qualified. The nominee accepting the committee's nomination must be consulted as it selects the nominees for other officers.

Elections
1. Officers shall be elected from the general assembly at the initial meeting of each school year.
2. If there is only one candidate for an office, election shall be by voice vote.
3. If there is more than one candidate for an office, election shall be by ballot.
4. A majority vote of the members present shall constitute an election.
5. Election of new officers shall take place at the general membership meeting in [month].
6. Elected officers shall serve a term of one year beginning [date] and ending [date] of the following year.
7. They shall be elected annually and installed at the [month] meeting to take office at the [month] meeting.

8. Officers are to be elected at the [month] meeting and shall assume their duties immediately following the close of that meeting.

Duties of the President
1. The president shall be in communication with the music director and all other officers of the organization.
2. The president shall have supervision over the business affairs of the association.
3. The president shall act as judge of all elections and declare results.
4. The president shall cast a deciding vote in case of a tie.
5. The president shall be chairman of the executive committee.
6. The president shall preside at all executive and general meetings and maintain order.
7. The president shall enforce a strict observance of the constitution and bylaws of the association.
8. The president shall put all questions, when seconded, to a vote.
9. The president shall direct the secretary to call special meetings of the organization or have the power to do so himself or herself.
10. The president shall appoint all standing and special committee chairs deemed necessary to fulfill the business and activities of the organization subject to the approval of the executive committee.
11. The president shall appoint an audit committee to audit the books of the organization at the end of the fiscal year.
12. The president shall serve ex officio on all committees except the nominating committee.
13. The president shall sign all vouchers along with the treasurer.
14. The president shall represent the association at any meeting the association delegates invite him or her to attend.
15. The president shall be available for advice and counsel during the year following the completion of his or her term of office, at which time he or she shall have a consultation session with the incoming president and turn over all appropriate files, reports, and keys.

Duties of the Vice President
1. The vice president is president elect and shall become president the following year.
2. The vice president shall carry out such specialized duties as are required for any particular school music group.
3. The vice president shall perform the duties of the president in the absence of the president.
4. Upon resignation of the president, the vice president shall fill the office of president until a special election can be held.
5. The vice president shall be in charge of parliamentary procedure.
6. The vice president shall work with the individual music directors and chairs of each school in the fitting of uniforms, robes, and other costumes.
7. The vice president shall chair the nominating committee.
8. The vice president shall act in the capacity of coordinator for all fundraising activities and secure necessary permits for such activities. In this capacity, he or she shall serve as chair of the ways and means committee.
9. The vice president shall assume the responsibility of soliciting advertising for football programs and program sales.

Constitution and Bylaws

10. The vice president shall be chair of the trip committee.
11. The vice president shall distribute any literature or materials at meetings that are pertinent to planned discussion.
12. The vice president shall prepare a final, written report of all his or her activities and duties, which shall be given to the president upon completion of his or her term of office.

Duties of the Secretary
1. The secretary shall attend all meetings and act as clerk thereof, and record all votes and minutes of all its transactions.
2. The secretary shall keep a copy of the bylaws.
3. The recording secretary shall keep records and minutes of all meetings.
4. The corresponding secretary shall attend to all routine correspondence.
5. On instructions from the president, the secretary shall conduct all correspondence for the association including the sending of appropriate thank-you notes.
6. Copies of all correspondence shall immediately be given to the president.
7. The secretary shall keep a correct record of the proceedings of all meetings of the organization and executive committee.
8. A copy of these recordings is to be given to each member of the executive committee and to the director of each music organization within a week of each meeting.
9. The secretary shall present a written report of minutes at all regular meetings, including a record of all attendees.
10. The secretary shall maintain a record of all dues-paying members.
11. The secretary shall present to the association a written record of those members eligible to vote in the next election.
12. The secretary shall notify those elected to office within ten days of their elections.
13. The secretary shall appraise committee members of their appointments.
14. The secretary shall be provided with a correct list of all members by the membership chairperson.
15. The secretary is responsible for all correspondence and shall perform other duties assigned by the president and the executive committee.
16. The secretary shall keep a file of all recordings, communications, and flyers.
17. The secretary shall read and answer all correspondence and shall have custody of the same.
18. The secretary shall secure all permits in advance to reserve rooms for meetings.
19. Upon leaving office, the secretary shall transmit all property of the organization entrusted to him or her to his or her successor.
20. The secretary's final written report of all duties performed shall be given to the president upon completion of term of office, along with the "secretary book" and all papers of the association.

Duties of the Treasurer
1. The treasurer shall be chair of the budget committee and be responsible for presenting the budget to the general board for review and for presenting the budget for adoption at the first general meeting of the fiscal year.
2. The treasurer shall file appropriate tax forms as necessary to preserve the tax-exempt status of the association.
3. The treasurer shall be bonded.

4. The treasurer shall receive all funds due the association, issue appropriate receipts, be solely responsible for deposit of funds in a designated depository determined by the board, and shall pay all bills upon authorization of the board. Checks may be signed by the president, vice president, or treasurer. Two signatures are required on each check.
5. The treasurer shall be the custodian of all monies and dues of the organization, recording the same in a bound ledger.
6. The treasurer shall pay all orders when presented to him or her and approved by the organization.
7. The treasurer shall maintain correct accounts of all monies and shall make deposits and payments designated by the executive committee.
8. The treasurer shall keep account of funds held by individual students and carry said accounts over from year to year.
9. The treasurer shall give a complete financial report at each meeting.
10. At all meetings, the treasurer shall submit a written report to the president and secretary. The report shall include beginning balance of the association's accounts, itemized income, interest earned, status of certificates held, itemized expenses, and ending balance. A copy should be filed with the president by the fifteenth of each month or as soon thereafter as bank statements are received.
11. Records will be audited at the end of the school year.
12. The treasurer shall prepare a summary of finances at the end of the fiscal year, which shall be available to all association members. Included in the report shall be an itemization of expenses and profits from each fundraising activity.
13. The treasurer shall sign all vouchers along with the president.
14. In an emergency and on approval of the president or vice president, the treasurer can disperse funds up to a limit of one hundred dollars. Such disbursements shall be reported to the association at the next state meeting.
15. Any two elected officers can authorize emergency expenditures up to fifty dollars.
16. During summer months, the treasurer shall pay any bill of two hundred dollars or less when so ordered by the majority of the executive committee without the approval of the general membership.
17. All disbursements will be made by check and all deposits in the name "_____ Music Boosters".

Vacancies
1. In case of a vacancy in the office of president, the vice president shall serve for the unexpired term.
2. In the event of a vacancy in an elective office, the executive committee may fill an unexpired term by appointment.
3. Elected offices vacated during the year shall be filled upon nomination by the president and upon approval of the executive board.
4. Any office vacated for any reason during the term must be filled by special election.
5. Any officer or committee chairman may be removed by a two-thirds vote of the executive board.
6. Any officer or agent may be removed by the board of directors whenever in its judgment the best interests of the corporation will be served thereby, but such removal shall be without prejudice to the contract rights of any person so removed.

Article III: Meetings
General Meetings
1. The general meeting of the organization shall be held on the [specify day] of each month from September to May [or specify months] beginning at [time] P.M. unless otherwise directed by the organization or the executive committee.
2. Two to three regular meetings of the membership shall be held each year, the time and place of said meetings to be determined by the executive committee.
3. The last meeting of the school year shall be known as the annual meeting at which time annual reports shall be received and officers for the following year shall be elected.
4. The music directors are to encourage attendance by making suitable announcements.
5. Public notices shall be made of all meetings.
6. A vote of a quorum of the executive committee, made not less than two weeks in advance, may alter the date of the regular meeting.
7. Scheduled meetings may be changed by the executive committee.
8. In the event of a schedule conflict with a music department program, a meeting may be rescheduled.
9. Meetings shall be open to all members.

Special Meetings
1. Special meetings may be called by the president at any time or by a majority of the executive committee.
2. Special meetings may be called at the discretion of the executive committee or the music director.
3. Special meetings may be called upon the written request of [number] members of the association.
4. May be called by the executive committee or by a petition signed by at least 10 percent of the membership of the association. Such petition shall state the purpose(s) for which the meeting is called.
5. All members are to receive notification for such meetings stating the purpose of the meeting.
6. No other business may be transacted than that for which the special meeting was called.
7. Business transacted at all special meetings shall be confined to the objects stated in the call and matters germane thereto.

Quorum
1. A meeting of members duly called shall not be organized for the transaction of business unless a quorum is present.
2. The members present at a duly organized meeting can continue to do business until adjournment, notwithstanding the withdrawal of enough members to leave less than a quorum.
3. A quorum shall be constituted by [percentage] of the membership.
4. [Number] members of this association shall constitute a quorum.
5. The presence, in person, of a majority of the members entitled to vote shall constitute a quorum.
6. Notice may be given ten days in advance that members present will constitute a quorum for the purpose of acting upon specific resolutions.
7. Members present constitute a quorum.

8. [Number] active members, to include one member of the executive committee, assembled at the time and place of the meeting shall constitute a quorum.
9. [Number] officers and [number] chairmen of standing committees and all present will constitute a quorum.
10. The assembled members at a regular or special meeting of this association shall constitute a quorum.
11. A simple majority of the members present and voting shall be sufficient to carry a motion.

Executive Committee Meetings
1. Executive committee meetings shall be held at the call of the president or a majority of the executive committee.
2. Executive committee meetings may be called by any member of the executive board upon agreement of the majority of the executive board.
3. Executive committee meetings shall be held at any time by call of the president, music director, or any three members.
4. Executive committee meetings shall be held when necessary.
5. Executive committee meetings shall be held on the [specific day] of each month.
6. Executive committee meetings shall be held in [specific months].
7. All members shall be given reasonable prior notice by the secretary regarding the time, place, and purpose of an executive committee meeting.
8. A report of business transacted at each executive meeting shall be made by the president at the following meeting of the general membership.
9. [Number] executive committee members shall constitute a quorum at executive committee meetings.
10. A majority of the members of the executive committee shall constitute a quorum.
11. A simple majority of the members present and voting shall be sufficient to carry a motion.

Order of Business
1. Call to order
2. Pledge of Allegiance
3. Secretary's report
4. Treasurer's report
5. Committee reports, music director, coordinators
6. Unfinished business
7. Old business
8. New business
9. Adjournment

Parliamentary Procedure
1. The latest edition of Robert's Rules of Order, Revised shall govern the organization in all cases to which they are applicable and not inconsistent with any provision of these bylaws.
2. Parliamentary law shall be the official guide for the association on all matters where this constitution and these bylaws are silent. The presiding officer shall, however, retain the authority to alter the order and procedures as he/she deems appropriate.
3. The aforementioned constitution and bylaws shall govern the music boosters association.
4. The music director shall act as parliamentarian.

Article IV: Committees
Executive Committee or Board
1. The elected officers of the organization, standing committee chairs, the immediate past president, and the music director(s) shall constitute the executive board.
2. The elected officers constitute the executive committee.
3. The board shall consist of all the elected officers of the association, plus four members appointed by the president. All music organizations from all schools must be represented.
4. The student president(s) of the [performing group or groups] shall also be included as a voting member(s) of the executive committee.
5. The board shall meet one week before the stated general meeting.
6. The board shall meet at the discretion of the president.
7. The purpose of the executive committee shall be to facilitate business at general meetings. This shall include the following:
   a. To review the plans and activities of the various other committees.
   b. To evaluate the plans of the ways and means committee for fundraising projects and to select and present appropriate options to the membership for approval or modification.
   c. To recommend to the general membership specific expenditures either for the operation of the organization or for the benefit of the [performing group], in keeping with the guidelines of the annual budget.
   d. To recommend to the general membership modifications to the annual budget approved at the [month] meeting.

General Committee Guidelines
1. Standing committees are those that function year-round or that have significant impact upon total operation of boosters. These committees shall include: auditing and finance, budget, bylaws, chaperon, communications, hospitality, liaison, membership, newsletter, program, publicity, social, student account, telephone, trip, transportation, uniform/robe, and ways and means. These shall consist of members from the general membership and shall not be limited in number.
2. Special committees may be established by the president for specific assignments from time to time throughout the year. These may include: awards, bake sale, band camp advisory, banquet, Christmas party, contest, cookies, festival, jacket, refreshment stand, trailer, and all special projects.
3. A chairman for each committee shall be appointed by the president with the approval of the executive committee. Terms shall be for one year, and any organization member is eligible to serve. A chairman shall have general supervision of the committee, shall hold meetings and conduct business when necessary, and shall submit a report to the executive committee periodically and present a report at each general meeting.

Auditing Committee
1. There shall be an auditing committee consisting of three members appointed by the president to audit the books of the treasurer each year at the end of the school term.
2. Upon completion of the audit, the auditing committee shall submit its report to the executive committee.
3. The auditing committee will audit the books at least twice during the year and also at the close of the club year.

4. The auditing committee shall develop and submit a proposal to the executive board each year for the adequate and continuous insurance coverage for the organization and all of its activities.
5. An independent, professional auditor shall be contracted from outside the organization.

Budget Committee
1. The budget committee shall consist of the music director(s), elected officers, and the chairman of the ways and means committee.
2. The budget committee shall prepare and submit to the organization a proposed budget at the first regular meeting of the school year.

Bylaws and Constitution Committee
1. The bylaws and constitution committee shall consist of three members to review the constitution and bylaws once a year and recommend changes deemed necessary.
2. The chairman will serve as organization parliamentarian.

Chaperon Committee
1. The chaperon committee shall enlist parents to act as chaperons for any music activity as deemed necessary by the music director(s).

Hospitality Committee
1. The hospitality committee shall assist in making meetings interesting and helpful.
2. The hospitality committee shall act as hosts at all general meetings, greeting guests and members.

Membership Committee
1. The membership committee shall solicit members, collect dues, issue membership cards, and keep a record of meeting attendance.
2. The membership committee shall consist of a parent member from each school or group supported by the organization.

Newsletter Committee
1. The newsletter committee shall gather, publish, and distribute all important information about the activities, accomplishments, and projects of the music organizations, their members, and the boosters.

Nominating Committee
1. The chair of the membership committee shall serve as chair of the nominating committee, and all chairs of standing committees shall be members, along with three members-at-large to be appointed by the president.
2. The nominating committee shall consist of four members, with one having been designated as chair and at least two representing the general membership (not on the executive board), all appointed by the president.
3. The music director(s) shall serve on this committee.
4. The nominating committee shall consist of three members: one from the executive committee and two from the association.
5. The nominating committee shall consist of one executive board member, one parent of an outgoing or graduating student, and one parent of an active student.
6. The nominating committee shall be elected by the executive board.

Publicity Committee
1. The publicity committee shall handle publicity related to the activities of the music boosters.

2. The publicity committee shall have a member from each school supported by the boosters.

Social Committee
1. In conjunction with the music director(s), the social committee shall assist in organizing and financing social activities for students in performing group(s).
2. The social committee shall plan events for boosters, such as picnics or dinner dances.

Student Account Committee
1. The student account committee shall assist the music director(s) in maintaining records of student financial accounts.

Telephone Committee
1. The telephone committee shall coordinate telephone notification of school music and organization activities to the membership.

Travel Committee
1. Under guidance of the music director(s), the travel committee shall investigate, plan, and arrange the details of trips by the music ensembles.
2. The travel committee shall work in close cooperation with the music director(s).

Uniform/Robe Committee
1. The uniform/robe committee shall assist the music director(s) in maintaining records of student uniform numbers, in distributing uniforms, and in the general maintenance and fitting of uniforms, robes, and other special costumes.

Ways and Means Committee
1. The ways and means committee shall recommend those ways of raising funds necessary for financing the activities of the booster organization and shall coordinate and implement them upon approval of the membership.
2. The chairman of the ways and means committee shall keep records of suppliers, project evaluations, and all monies.
3. The chairman of the ways and means committee shall appoint the chairs of all special fundraising projects.

Committee Finances
1. Any committee may be given a monetary advance to set up a project by majority action of the executive committee.
2. Committees engaging in fundraising projects or entering into contracts must have approval by a majority of the executive committee before the organization's name may be used or for financial obligations incurred.
3. All bills for expenses incurred by a committee should be approved promptly by the committee chairman and forwarded to the treasurer so that vouchers may be prepared for payment.

Article V: Finances

1. The association is tax exempt and shall make every effort to maintain its status as a tax-exempt organization.
2. In addition to the treasurer, all persons of the music boosters association handling monies shall be bonded.
3. Monies or funds raised by, for, or in the name of the [performing group] under the sponsorship of the music boosters association become the property of the music boosters association.

4. Such funds are to be used only to cover minimal operating expenses and to support approved projects, activities, and programs of the [performing group].
5. All monies collected by this organization shall be for the use of the spring tour of the [performing group].
6. The fiscal year shall be from [date] to [date].
7. Student account records, when maintained, are to record each student's earned contribution toward trips or other planned student activities. Funds recorded in these accounts are NOT the property of individual students and may not be refunded.
8. Monies shall never be returned to the student, passed down to a younger sibling, or refunded in any manner.
9. In the event a student moves, graduates, or quits the organization, the monies become a part of the general fund of the music boosters association.
10. Parent contributions to support for student earned activities will be recorded as such.
11. The association encourages selling through the fundraising program. Four options are available to students:
    a. A student, by selling, may pay for the entire trip (quota plus parent assessment).
    b. a student, by selling, may pay the quota. Parents pay the parent assessment.
    c. A student, by selling, may pay part of the quota. Parents pay the difference plus the parent assessment, plus an additional amount beyond these two. This additional amount will be given to the student at the time of the trip.
    d. Parents pay entire amount—quota, parent assessment, plus an additional amount to be determined for each trip.
12. Built into the fundraising tracking system is an amount from each sale that goes directly into the association's general fund. This fund provides additional benefits for the students (such as awards, banquets, and activities) and underwrites the general expenses of the organization.
13. All monies credited to a student but not used toward a trip for a legitimate reason (legitimacy to be determined by the music director) shall be carried over in the name of that student until the end of his/her senior year or until the end of his or her attendance at the school. At that time such monies shall revert to the general treasury of the boosters, except that if the student has a younger brother or sister in the music program, said monies shall be credited to him or her in an equitable manner.
14. A vote will be taken each year to determine if the boosters will pay the expenses for any student attending honors, district, regional, or state festivals.

Article VI: Awards

1. The association shall recognize any student selected to perform at any county music festival.
2. The association shall award [dollar amount] to top seniors in band, orchestra, and chorus, as selected by the directors. The students' names shall be engraved on a hall plaque.
3. Outstanding [grade] band, orchestra, and chorus members shall receive trophies and have their names engraved on a school plaque.
4. The association shall award a scholarship, the amount of which will be voted on every year. The awardee must be registered as an instrumental/vocal music major at college.

5. The association shall award a yearly scholarship, the amount of which will be decided by a committee comprising the director, the president of the booster association, and an administrator to further a senior's education.
6. The association shall underwrite sweater and letter awards. These awards require at least two years of membership. "Membership" shall be construed to include band or chorus service prior to moving into the district.
7. A letter shall be awarded to any senior not eligible for a sweater and letter award.
8. Band ribbons shall be awarded for the current year after band camp.
9. An individual recognition dinner shall be given to any student who distinguishes himself or herself above and beyond regular service, for example, in county, district, or regional events.
10. Decisions on awardees shall be made by boosters and music director.
11. Awards shall be funded by ways and means committee projects.

Article VII: Dissolution

1. Upon dissolution or disbandment of this association, any and all unallocated cash funds shall be turned over to the school for exclusive use in the music programs.

Article VIII: Standing Rules

1. All matters pertaining to the activities, events, and projects of the [performing group] and the music parents association must meet with the approval of the music director and must be in keeping with the policy of the school district.
2. The association shall maintain a post office box for the purpose of having an address and receiving mail. The keys to said box shall be retained by the president and the treasurer.
3. Equipment of the organization is not to be lent to any persons or organizations for use outside of the school buildings or grounds.
4. Each member shall have an equal right to speak on all matters brought before the association.
5. Persons granted the right to speak will give their names.
6. No matters will be discussed that originate outside the association. All matters will be introduced by an association member.
7. Political speakers will not be allowed to occupy the time of the association.
8. Should any grievance arise within the association, the executive committee, and/or the school music personnel representative, the following steps shall be taken:
    a. The grievance shall be specified in writing and to the person involved at a regular meeting.
    b. The grievance shall be taken to the school administration.
    c. The grievance shall be taken to the board of education.

Article IX: Amendments

1. Any proposed changes or amendments shall be submitted in writing to the executive committee thirty days prior to a regular meeting, at which time they will be voted upon.
2. These bylaws shall be read at the [specify] meeting and shall be reviewed for revision every [number] years beginning with the year 19__.
3. This constitution may be amended at any regular meeting of the organization by a [fraction or percentage] vote, provided that the secretary has given [number] days

written notice, including the full text of the proposed amendment, to the full membership.
4. All resolutions, with the names of the persons making the motion and seconding, must be presented in writing in correct form to the secretary of the executive committee.
5. All resolutions must be approved a majority vote.
6. All resolutions must be approved by a majority vote, provided there are at least [number] members present.

Appendix 2
Uniform Management

The uniform committee can provide valuable assistance in issuing and maintaining uniforms. For legal reasons it is especially advisable for parents to be responsible for measuring students prior to distribution. The most important aspect of managing uniform supplies is to identify each component in the inventory. Records should be kept on the use of all items and the maintenance expense. This is most valuable in budgeting for replacements and damaged items. It also provides the basis for a uniform rental fee when necessary.

MASTER PROPERTY LISTS

The accompanying uniform property list is recommended for keeping record of major components of the uniforms. Parts such as pants, coats, and hats will have an identification number sewn in by the manufacturer. Each component of the uniform should be listed separately in size order to expedite assignment. Coats tailored for males and females should be listed separately. When listing pants, the original length and waist size should be recorded. Pant legs should never be cut. Make adjustments by hemming, turning the excess up inside the pant leg.

UNIFORM PROPERTY LIST

Uniform Item	Identification Number	Acquisition Date	Acquisition Cost	Size	Issue Record 19__	19__	19__

MUSIC BOOSTER MANUAL

The accompanying miscellaneous property list is recommended for consumable items (those with a relatively high turnover rate) that are not dependent on size for issue. Examples include spats, plumes for hats, and braids or other decorative items.

MISCELLANEOUS PROPERTY LIST

Item	Identification	Acquisition		Quantitiy	Issued	Return	Remarks
		Date	Cost				

The accompanying issue/use record is the working control for items issued from the inventory. It is individualized for each student and includes his or her measurements and components or equipment issued. Uniform rental fee records can also be annotated on the form. Summarize available uniform components on the accompanying uniform assignment chart.

ISSUE/USE RECORD

NAME: _____   PHONE NO:_____

Year	Year	Year
Waist____ Height____ Chest____ Weight____ Head____ Inseam____	Waist____ Height____ Chest____ Weight____ Head____ Inseam____	Waist____ Height____ Chest____ Weight____ Head____ Inseam____
Issue Record	Issue Record	Issue Record
Return Condition_____	Return Condition_____	Return Conditon_____

ASSIGNING UNIFORMS

If possible, measure students about two to three weeks before uniforms are to be issued.
  Chest. Place tape horizontally around the body close under the arms and check to see that it is centered well over shoulder blades in back and over fullest part of the breast in front. Do not draw tape too tightly or allow it to sag.

PERFORMANCE SUPPORT

If the music director requests it, members of the uniform committee or boosters familiar with the required appearance for each type of uniform can conduct an inspection. They should see that each uniform is complete and is being worn properly.

Develop a kit to take care of repairs or replacements. This kit should be on hand any time an inspection is held, and it should be taken on all trips made by the performing group. The kit should contain a complete replacement for each type of uniform worn, and several spare small items (such as buttons, belts, gloves, spats, collars, stoles, and braids). Medium to large sizes are recommended because missing or damaged parts can be swapped down in size. Collect spares or adjust uniform records to reflect the changes.

MAINTENANCE

The appearance and life of any uniform is greatly affected by how well it is maintained. Implement control measures to ensure periodic cleaning, repairs, and preventive maintenance. Have uniforms cleaned regularly and prior to storage at the end of a performing season. Make arrangements with a local cleaner for a quantity discount.

When uniforms are turned in for storage at the conclusion of the season, they should be carefully inspected for necessary repairs. Repair work should be completed before the uniforms are cleaned and stored. When uniforms are issued, provide care and maintenance instructions to students and parents. Instructions should cover cleaning requirements, replacement costs for damaged or lost parts, and the group's policy on rental fees and deposits.

Waist. Measure around waist just above trouser waistband over the shirt. Do not measure over vest, belt, or waistband. Do not allow tape to sag.

Trouser inseam. Adjust trousers to waist position where uniform is customarily worn. Place end of tape in crotch at crotch seam and measure to desired length. The measurement should be taken with the student wearing shoes that will be worn with the uniform or shoes that have the same size heels.

Hat. Measure the head with the hair styled as it will be with the hat and at the position where the hatband will rest. Use the following chart to convert head measurements in inches to hat sizes.

Inches	Hat Size	Inches	Hat Size
19	6	22-3/8	7-1/8
19-3/8	6-1/8	22-3/4	7-1/4
19-3/4	6-1/4	23-1/8	7-3/8
20-1/8	6-3/8	23-1/2	7-1/2
20-1/2	6-1/2	23-7/8	7-5/8
20-7/8	6-5/8	24-1/4	7-3/4
21-1/4	6-3/4	24-5/8	7-7/8
21-5/8	6-7/8	25	8
22	7		

Summarize size measurements for each component on the uniform assignment chart. The size column is for sizes of a particular uniform part. The quantity line represents the total available in the inventory for that size. When the measurement totals for the corresponding uniform parts are listed on the form, start the assignment process. The issue line is where you record any adjustment necessary to fit the available parts to the students. Start with the smallest size and work any adjustments upward. Use a pencil when recording the initial issue. When all uniforms are issued and exchanges made, enter the student's name under the year column of the master property lists.

If inventory and student measurements are entered in a computer data base, sorting uniform components and students by size can be done much more quickly. Worksheets and final lists can be printed out with data arranged any number of ways. Information can be updated and reprinted easily at any time.

UNIFORM ASSIGNMENT CHART

ITEM_____

Size									
Quantity									
Survey									
Issue									

www.ingramcontent.com/pod-product-compliance
Lightning Source LLC
Chambersburg PA
CBHW082207230426
43672CB00015B/2926